英語
療癒筆記

每天手寫10分鐘的幸福時光

李寶寧——著　　韓蔚笙——譯

全書音檔線上聽

Everything's going to be okay.

一切都會好起來的。

大家好，我是李寶寧。

我想向各位坦白一件事。其實我與外表看起來不同，個性謹小慎微，相當怕生、容易害羞，也非常害怕受到傷害。由於這種性格與社會大眾對我的期許不同，讓我深感無力，經常獨自痛苦煩惱。於是，從某個瞬間開始，每當有心煩意亂的事情發生時，我便會藉由寫日記來平復自己的心情。使我感到疲憊的事、讓我得到安慰的事、從明天開始重新出發的決心，以及賦予我力量的良言佳句等，即便只是寫下一行，也足以讓心情放鬆。無需在意別人的看法，單純只為自己而書寫鼓舞的文字，這賦予我極大的力量，支持我長期作為英語教育家持續進行各種活動。因此，我產生了一個念頭，如果有一天我能用這些讓我獲得勇氣的文字，幫助別人就好了。

在漫長的英語教學生涯中，我遇過許許多多的人。無論是兒童、學生、上班族、家長、求職者或是年長者，每個人都懷抱著各自的煩惱。這本書是我寫給儘管懷抱著煩惱，仍每天努力生活的各位之應援信。根據我自己的經驗，我想告訴各位，即使偶爾因為看著別人而感到嫉妒、受傷、憤怒、焦躁和怨恨，這一切面貌也是我們必須擁抱的，屬於自己的一部分，我們並不會因此而一敗塗地。

You are enough, just as you are.

你原來的樣貌就已經夠好了。

　　雖然現今社會變得比從前更加開放，但另一方面，我卻認為人與人之間築起了比任何時候都還要厚的心防。然而，在寫這本書時，我花了更多時間靜靜地審視自己與自己身邊的人，在此過程中，我感受到難以言喻的慰藉與療癒。因此，我懇切地希望能將這種心靈上的寧靜傳達給更多人。

　　請每天抽出十分鐘的時間。只要閱讀、聆聽並跟著抄寫能為各位帶來慰藉和勇氣的話語，就能尋得內心的平靜以及片刻放鬆。我衷心希望這本書能夠成為一顆小小的維他命，讓疲憊不堪的我們在體會抄寫樂趣的同時，也能獲得一點點持續前行的力量。另外，英語學習也是不可或缺的，對吧？從四十則療癒訊息中選出實用的英語表達與句型，請各位不要有壓力，輕鬆地學習，您將同時獲得紮實的英語實力。

　　如此審視自己內心並寫成坦率的文字，比我所想的更加困難，因此加深了我的苦惱。每當這種時候，包括Darakwon編輯群在內眾多親朋好友的建議，都給予我極大的幫助。衷心感謝賜予我這個機會的所有人。

今天也在不斷尋求寬慰的
英語教育家　李寶寧敬上

目次

Capital Letters

A

B

C

D

E

F

G

H

I

J

K

L

M

N

O

P

Q

R

S

T

U

V

W

X

Y

Z

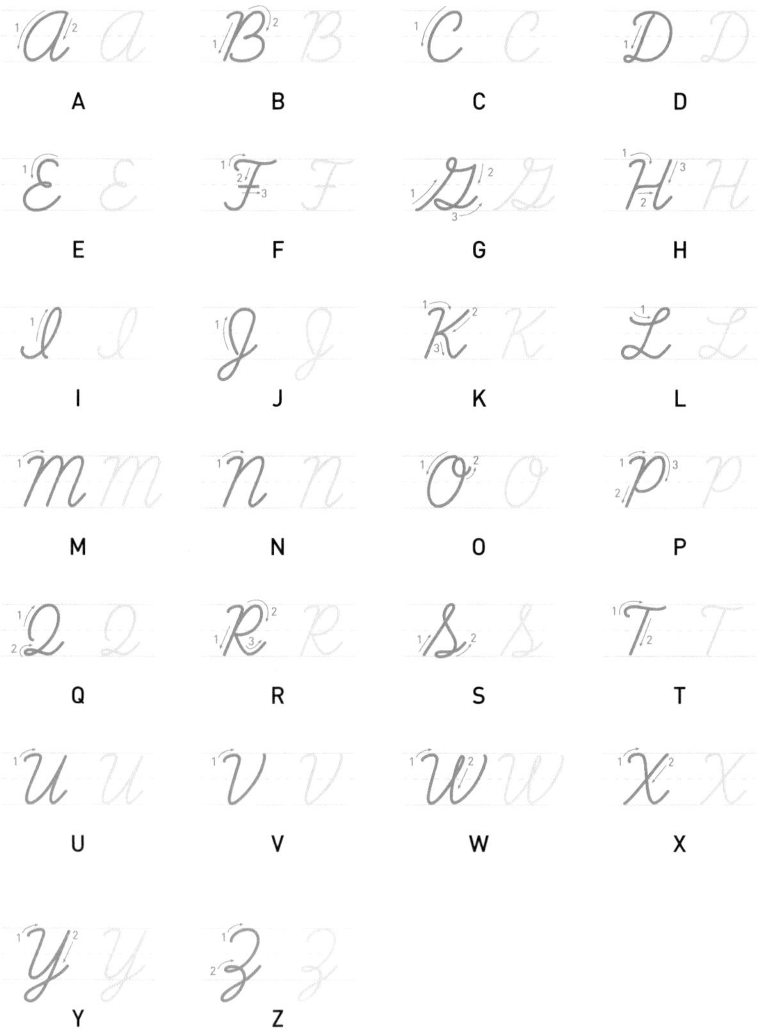

Small Letters

a

b

c

d

e

f

g

h

i

j

k

l

m

n

o

p

q

r

s

t

u

v

w

x

y

z

| **例言** |

本書中盡可能運用了母語人士於日常生活中常用的英語表達。另外,比起直譯每一個英語單字,更偏向以中文聽起來自然流暢的方式來解讀英語文句。希望各位在閱讀時,比起鑽研個別單字字義,能更專注於字裡行間所傳達的含意。

WEEK 1

今天也
辛苦了

DAY
01

一二三四五六日，
我的一週

On Monday,
I drag myself out of the bed and go off to work.
This long week of 7 days has just started,
and I feel worn out already.
But I will carry on through the week
looking forward to the weekend.
I know it will be Saturday in no time,
and I will cherish it in the sweetest way.
Yay, go for it!

星期一，我強迫自己起床去上班。
七天，漫長的一週才剛剛開始，
我卻已然感到精疲力盡。但我會努力撐過一星期，
堅持下去並期盼著週末的到來。週六將在轉瞬間來臨，
而我將盡情享受甜美的週末。
好，加油吧！

🌸 讀、聆聽、書寫

🌸 手寫體書寫

But I will carry on through the week looking forward to the weekend.

worn out 精疲力盡　　*cherish* 珍惜　　*go for* 為～而努力

I feel... already.

我已經覺得～

I feel hungry **already.**

我肚子已經餓了。

I feel sad **already.**

我已經開始難過了。

I feel excited **already.**

我已經感到興奮了。

I feel better **already.**

我的心情已經好多了。

I feel melancholy **already.**   *melancholy* 憂鬱的

我已經開始心情鬱悶了。

🌸 寫寫看

I feel   already.

14

Yay, go for it!

好，加油吧！

回家的路

Although this is the same old way
leading to my home,
somehow it feels a bit different today.
Maybe it's just me all worn out
from a long, hard day's work.
Only the moonlight seems to keep me company.
It is cheering me up and saying that I am a survivor.
I am a survivor. I've survived another day.
When I get home, I will wrap up the day by
celebrating with soul food and
my favorite TV show.

與往日相同的回家之路，今天不知為何感覺有些許不同。
或許只是因為度過了漫長而艱辛的一天，使我精疲力盡。
彷彿只有月光陪伴著我。
它為我加油打氣，說我是「堅持下來的生存者」。
我是挺過今天的人。我又戰勝了一天。
所以當我回到家時，我要吃最愛的食物，看最喜歡的電視節目，
在慶祝中為這一天畫下句點。

🌸 手寫體書寫

It is cheering me up and saying that I am a survivor. I am a survivor. I've survived another day.

company 陪伴　*survivor* 克服逆境的人、生存者　*wrap up* 結束

Maybe it's just me, ...
也許只有我這樣～

Maybe it's just me, but it's unusually cold today.

也許只有我這麼認為，但今天特別冷。

Maybe it's just me, but I feel so hungry already.

也許只有我這麼認為，但我肚子已經餓了。

Maybe it's just me, but I think the movie was a flop.

或許只有我這麼覺得，但我認為這部電影是個失敗的作品。

Maybe it's just me, but I think there's something wrong.

也許只有我這麼覺得，但我感覺有些不對勁。

Maybe it's just me, but I think there's someone in this house.

也許這只是我的想法，但這棟房子裡好像有其他人。

🌸 **寫寫看**

Maybe it's just me,

Only the moonlight
seems to keep me company.

彷彿只有月光陪伴著我。

每天為我帶來笑容的事物

Try keeping a daily record of things
that make you happy.
They can be about whatever
makes you smile that day.
It doesn't matter how trivial it may be.
Those little events matter:
like a flower you noticed on the street,
your subway train arrived right on time…
Count your small blessings and keep carrying on.
Who knows? Maybe tomorrow will add another
small wonder to make it a better day.

試著每天記錄讓你快樂的事物。
他們可以是任何那天為你帶來笑容的事物。
無論多麼微不足道也無所謂，因為那些小事也很珍貴。
例如，在街道旁發現的一朵花，或是你搭乘的地鐵準時抵達等等。
細數發生在你身上的小確幸，繼續努力生活下去。
誰知道呢？或許明天會再增添一個小驚喜，
讓它成為更美好的一天。

❀ 手寫體書寫

Who knows? Maybe tomorrow will add another small wonder to make it a better day.

trivial 瑣碎的　*matter* 重要、有關係　*notice* 察覺到　*carry on* 繼續下去

Try -ing...
試著去做～

Try learning English with this book.

試著用這本書學英語。

Try baking a cake.　*bake* 烘烤（糕點）

試著烤蛋糕。

Try exercising every day.

試著每天運動。

Try using this system.

試著使用此系統。

Try shopping online.

試試看線上購物。

 寫寫看

Try

Those little things that make you happy.

那些讓你開心的小事。

期待未知的明天

Who knows what tomorrow brings?
I may win the lotto.
My dearest friend may turn into my worst enemy.
Just the thought of it makes me scared.
But isn't that what makes life worth living?
Life is full of all kinds of surprises.
So I can't wait to find out
what tomorrow has in store for me.
See you all tomorrow.

沒有人知道明天會發生什麼事。
也許我會中樂透。
也許我最愛的朋友會成為我最可怕的敵人。
光是想像就令人害怕。
但正因如此，人生才有意義不是嗎？
生活充滿各式各樣的驚奇。
所以我非常好奇明天會發生什麼事。
我們明天見。

🌸 手寫體書寫

So I can't wait to find out what tomorrow has in store for me. See you all tomorrow.

turn into 變成　*in store for* 為～準備

Just the thought of it makes me...
光是想到就讓我～

Just the thought of it makes me sad.

光是想到就讓我感到難過了。

Just the thought of it makes me feel uncomfortable.

光是想到就讓我覺得不舒服。

Just the thought of it makes me sweat.

光是想到就令我冒汗。

Just the thought of it makes me nervous.

光是想到我就開始緊張了。

Just the thought of it makes me angry.

光是想到就令我生氣。

 寫寫看

Just the thought of it makes me

Who knows what tomorrow brings?
Life is full of all kinds of surprises.

沒有人知道明天會發生什麼事。
生活充滿各式各樣的驚奇。

感恩的心

I am thankful…
to the man at work for holding the elevator for me;
to my friend for getting me a nice coffee;
to the bus driver for responding nicely to my *hello*.
Every day, we can be grateful to someone or something
for a good reason.
Recalling at least three such things
shouldn't be that hard.
**Besides, gratitude will completely change
your day and your life as a whole.**

感謝為我按住電梯的公司員工。
感謝買好喝咖啡給我的朋友。
感謝親切回應我問候的公車司機。
我們每天都會基於各種緣由，對某人或某事心存感激。
回想三件以上這樣的事情應該不難。
而且，感恩的心將徹底改變你的日常生活與人生。

❀ 手寫體書寫

Besides, gratitude will completely change your day and your life as a whole.

grateful 感激的　recall 記起　gratitude 感激之情、感謝

I am thankful to...
我很感謝～

I am thankful to my parents.

我很感謝我的父母。

I am thankful to my colleagues.　*colleague* 公司同事

我很感謝我的同事們。

I am thankful to the readers of this book.

感謝這本書的讀者們。

I am thankful to my subscribers.　*subscriber* 訂閱者、付費會員

很感謝我的訂閱者們。

I am thankful to my friends.

感謝我的朋友們。

 寫寫看

I am thankful to

Every day,
we can be grateful
to someone
or something
for a good reason.

每天，
我們都會基於各種緣由，
對某人或某事心存感激。

-》》》 *Thank You* 《《《-

今天也謝謝你

仔細環顧四周,你會發現一天內發生許多值得感謝的事。
請試著寫下你今天要感謝的對象。

我今天要感謝 ＿＿＿＿＿＿＿＿＿＿＿ 。

- 總是先熱情向我打招呼的公司同事

- 朋友送我一杯溫暖的茶

- 順利完成一天工作的自己

-

-

WEEK 2

時間為我們
解決的事

無論再辛苦，
終將成為過去

◆ ◆ ◆

This, too, shall pass.
Everything is fleeting.
Either good or bad.
Looking back, you may feel that
everything seems so small and frivolous.
Why waste your breath over it?
There's no need to hold grudges.

⚜

這也終將過去的。
不論是好事還是壞事，
一切皆如浮光掠影。
當你回首時，或許會認為一切都如此渺小且無關緊要。
所以何必為這種小事浪費精力呢？
而且也沒必要耿耿於懷。

_____

_____

_____

_____

_____

_____

_____

_____

_____

🌸 **手寫體書寫**

This, too, shall pass. Everything is fleeting.

Either good or bad.

_____

_____

fleeting 轉瞬即逝的　*frivolous* 無關緊要的
waste one's breath 浪費力氣、白費唇舌　*grudge* 嫌隙、怨恨

There's no need to...

沒必要～

There's no need to complain.

沒必要抱怨。

There's no need to hurry.

沒必要著急。

There's no need to hesitate.

無需猶豫不決。

There's no need to wait any longer.

不需要再等下去了。

There's no need to buy so much water now.

現在不需要買那麼多水。

 寫寫看

There's no need to

This, too, shall pass.

這也終將過去的。

門前的恐懼毫無力量

◆ ◆ ◆

Am I scared? What am I scared of?
If I can fight back,
I will gladly take on the challenge.
If I don't feel like fighting back,
then I can just walk away.
Either way, I'm okay. **I always have options.**
90% of my worries don't really
even happen at all, they say.
**So I will just cross each bridge
when I come to it.**

·

我在害怕嗎？我在害怕什麼？
如果能夠反擊，我很樂意接受挑戰；
如果不想戰鬥，我也可以直接離開。
無論如何，我都會沒事。因為我永遠有選擇的餘地。
人們說，我擔心的事情有百分之九十根本不會發生。
所以如果煩惱成真，就到時候再來應對吧。

🌸 手寫體書寫

*I always have options. So I will just cross each
bridge when I come to it.*

fight back 反擊　　*take on* 承擔、接受　　*cross* 越過

I will gladly...
我很樂意～

I will gladly help you.

我很樂意幫助你。

I will gladly keep you company.

我很樂意陪在你身邊。

I will gladly be there for you.　　*be there for* 在～身邊成為力量

我很樂意在你身邊給你力量。

I will gladly take the offer.　　*offer* 提議

我很樂意接受這個提議。

I will gladly listen to your story.

我很樂意傾聽你的故事。

 寫寫看

I will gladly

No need to fear.
Open the door.

無需害怕。
打開門吧。

偶爾偷懶
也沒關係

• • •

Today was another lazy day.
Time went by so slowly.
I didn't feel like doing anything.
I wonder if that is a sin.
Not really.
It's not like I'm wasting my life at all.
**Rather, I'm just taking time to
listen to myself.**

•

今天又是慵懶的一天。
時間流動得真慢。我什麼事也不想做。
我很好奇,這是什麼天大的罪過嗎?
並非如此。
因為我並不是在浪費生命。
相反地,我空出時間,
來好好傾聽自己內心的聲音。

手寫體書寫

Rather, I'm just taking time to listen to
myself.

lazy 慵懶的　　*sin* 罪、錯誤　　*rather* 反而、相反地

I didn't feel like -ing...

我沒有心情做～

I didn't feel like cooking.

我沒有心情做飯。

I didn't feel like working out.　　*work out* 運動

我不想運動。

I didn't feel like calling him.

我不想打電話給他。

I didn't feel like going out.

我不太想出門。

I didn't feel like cleaning the house.

我沒有心情打掃房子。

 寫寫看

I didn't feel like

I'm just listening to myself.

我只是在傾聽自己內心的聲音。

斬斷緣份的時候

◆ ◆ ◆

I know the world is not filled only with angels.
Unfortunately, there are some
truly bad people out there, too.
I've never wanted to believe that,
but that is true.
So what can we do?
Just cut off those toxic people from your life.
Only then can we finally
start making new and better connections.

·

我也知道，
這世界上並非只有如同天使般善良的人。
不幸的是，世界上確實也有壞人存在。
雖然我不願意相信，但這就是事實。
所以我們該怎麼辦呢？
直接斬斷與對你人生有害之人的連結吧。
唯有如此，我們才能重新建立新的、更美好的關係。

🌸 手寫體書寫

Just cut off those toxic people from your life

---

unfortunately 遺憾的是、不幸的是　*toxic* 有毒的　*connection* 關係、連結

... be filled with...
充滿～

This room **is filled with** smoke.

這個房間煙霧瀰漫。

The book **is filled with** great stories.

那本書滿載著精彩的故事。

My heart **was filled with** excitement.

我的心中充滿興奮。

The air **was filled with** a terrible smell.   *terrible* 可怕的

空氣中充斥著惡臭。

The letter **was filled with** anger.

這封信中充斥著憤怒。

 寫寫看

filled with

*Life is C(choice) between
B(birth) and D(death).*

人生是由生與死之間，無數選擇所構成的。

• Jean Paul Sartre

逃跑是為了重新回來

◆ ◆ ◆

There are times when nothing seems to go right.
When you feel like letting your hair down
and forgetting about it all,
that's when you recharge yourself
for the next round.
So why don't you just switch off for a while
and get away from it all?
You'll come back tomorrow anyway.
**So just run, run away from it all today
so that you can come back in better shape
tomorrow.**

有時就是會覺得諸事不順。
當你想要放下一切、忘記所有時，
便是該為下一輪比賽充電做準備的時候了。
因此，何不暫時關掉電源並遠離這一切呢？
反正你明天還會再回來。
所以今天就跑走，逃離這一切吧。
如此明天才能以更好的狀態回歸。

🌸 手寫體書寫

So just run, run away from it all today so that you can come back in better shape tomorrow.

let one's hair down 放鬆休息　　*switch off* 關掉電源、停止關注
shape 形態、樣貌

You can...
你可以～

You can make a U-turn here.

你可以在這裡迴轉。

You can always come back.

你隨時都可以回來。

You can stay here as long as you want.

你想在這裡待多久都可以。

You can use any computer here.

你可以使用這裡任一台電腦。

You can ask the person at the info desk.

你可以詢問服務櫃台的人員。

 寫寫看

You can

So why don't you
just switch off for a while
and get away from it all?

因此，何不暫時關掉電源
並遠離這一切呢？

If I Could Travel in Time...
如果能夠搭乘時光機

如果能夠搭乘時光機，你想前往過去還是未來？
請自由地寫下前往那個時間點後，
你想做的事和想見的人。

- 請勾選你想前往的時間。

  過去　　　　　未來

- 具體時間點是什麼時候？

- 你為何想前往那個時間點？

- 你想在那裡見到誰？

- 你想在那裡做什麼事？

WEEK 3

從今天開始
愛自己

為嫉妒心所苦時

♦ ♦ ♦

When you look at other people's lives
on social media, what catches your eye first?
Their fancy bags and big cars?
Sometimes those pictures get me down,
leaving me green with envy.
But do I really need those things to live a good life?
**I am already a great person
who doesn't need those decorations
to look good.**

當你在社群媒體上觀看他人生活時,首先吸引你目光的是什麼?
是他們的昂貴皮包和豪華汽車嗎?
那樣的照片有時會使我心情低落,也會令我感到嫉妒。
然而,我真的需要那些奢侈品才能過上美好生活嗎?
我已經是個優秀的人了,
不需要那些裝飾品來襯托我的美好。

🌸 手寫體書寫

I am already a great person who doesn't need those decorations to look good.

fancy 高級的　*get ~ down* 讓～憂鬱、讓～心情低落
green with envy 非常嫉妒、眼紅

... get me down.
〜讓我心情低落

Sad movies **get me down.**

悲傷的電影使我心情低落。

Mean people **get me down.** *mean* 卑劣的、刻薄的

卑劣的人讓我感到無力。

Rainy days **get me down.**

下雨天讓我心情低落。

Cloudy weather **gets me down.**

多雲的天氣讓我提不起精神。

Tragic news **gets me down.**

悲慘的消息令我感到沮喪。

🌸 寫寫看

get me down.

If you want to get over jealousy,
just keep your eyes closed for a moment.

若想克服嫉妒心，就暫時閉上你的雙眼。

DAY 12

我自己選擇的甜蜜孤獨

Sometimes I feel like an island.
All the others seem so far away,
having their own little party.
It would be nice if I could mingle with them.
But for now,
I choose to be here on the outside,
fully enjoying my own little peace and quiet.
Me here and you there,
we keep cheering for each other.

有時，我覺得自己像一座孤島。
其他人都離我非常遙遠，
在開屬於他們自己的小派對。
若我能融入他們就好了，但現在我選擇待在外面。
充分享受只屬於我的小小平和與寧靜。
我在這裡，你在那裡，
我們一直為彼此加油。

🌸 手寫體書寫

But for now, I choose to be here on the outside,
fully enjoying my own little peace and quiet.

mingle 融入人群進行交談　*for now* 暫時、目前

It would be nice if I could...

如果我能～就好了

It would be nice if I could be there with you.

如果我能在那裡陪你就好了。

It would be nice if I could join you for dinner.

要是我能跟你一起享用晚餐就好了。

It would be nice if I could hang out with you.

如果我能跟你一起共度時光就好了。

It would be nice if I could have today off.

如果我今天能休息一天就好了。

It would be nice if I could go on a trip.

要是我能去旅行就好了。

 寫寫看

It would be nice if I could

sweet solitude

甜蜜的孤獨

DAY 13

認識自己的旅程

• ◆ •

"Know thyself," said Socrates.
What do I like the most? What do I hate the most?
What are some of my pet peeves?
**Exploring what kind of person I am
can be quite a journey.**
The answers are not to be easily found.
Along the journey, I shall be able to figure out
whom I can turn to.
Eventually, I will be a big enough person
to be fully responsible for my own choices.

「認識你自己」，蘇格拉底如是說。
我最喜歡什麼？我最討厭什麼？
令我厭煩到無法忍受的事物為何？探索我是個什麼樣的人，
將是一場壯闊的旅程。
解答無法被輕易尋得。
在這趟旅程中，我將明白誰才是我能依靠的人。
最終，我將成為一個有擔當的人，
足以對自己的選擇負責。

🌸 讀、聆聽、書寫

🌸 手寫體書寫

Exploring what kind of person I am can be quite a journey.

thyself 你自己　pet peeve 極度煩人的事物　turn to 依靠、求助於

What do... the most?
最～的是什麼？

What do you want **the most?**
你最想要的是什麼？

What do you miss **the most?**
你最想念的是什麼？

What do you not like **the most?**
你最不喜歡的是什麼？

What do you want to do **the most?**
你最想做的是什麼？

What do you enjoy **the most?**
你最享受的是什麼？

 寫寫看

What do   the most?

I want to know myself.

我想認識「我自己」。

愛自己比想像的更難

◆ ◆ ◆

Loving myself and taking myself as I am
might not be as easy as it sounds.
On the contrary, you might find it
easier to love others.
I'm not saying we should love every bit of ourselves
no matter what.
Rather, we need to focus on our strengths,
face the consequences,
and believe in and root for ourselves.
That is my idea of loving myself.

愛自己並接受自己原本的模樣，或許沒有聽起來那般容易。
反之，你可能會覺得愛別人更簡單。
我並不是說我們必須無條件地愛自己的每一面。
而是要更專注於自己的優點，
直面結果，相信自己並為自己加油打氣。
我認為這就是愛自己的方式。

🌸 讀、聆聽、書寫

🌸 手寫體書寫

Rather, we need to focus on our strengths, face the consequences, and believe in and root for ourselves.

strength 優點　*face* 面對　*consequence* 結果　*root for ~* 為～加油打氣、支持

That is my idea of...
那就是我對於～的看法

That is my idea of enjoying vacation.

我認為那就是享受假期的方式。

That is my idea of taking care of ourselves.

我對於照顧好我們自己的看法。

That is my idea of working hard.

那就是我對於努力工作的看法。

That is my idea of having fun.

那就是我對於開心玩耍的看法。

That is my idea of having a great weekend.

那就是我想像中度過美好周末的方式。

 寫寫看

That is my idea of

I like myself.
I'm an interesting person.

我喜歡我自己。
我是個有趣的人。

現在需要做的事

◆ ◆ ◆

Stop comparing myself to others.
Stop saying, "I knew I couldn't do it.
What did I expect?"
Slouch no more. Keep looking straight ahead.
Write down my 3 biggest strengths.
Think of the ones who love me.
Set up a weekly plan.
Mark on the map the places
that I'd love to visit someday.
Turn off the phone and TV
and just listen to my inner voice.

停止與他人比較。
不要再說：「我就知道我無法做到。我到底在期待些什麼？」
不要垂頭喪氣、持續直視前方。
寫下我三個最大的優點。
想想那些愛我的人們。
制定一週計劃。
在地圖上標示總有一天要去的地方。
關掉手機和電視，專心聆聽內心的聲音。

🌸 手寫體書寫

Stop comparing myself to others. Slouch no more. Keep looking straight ahead.

compare 比較　*slouch* 垂頭喪氣、彎腰駝背

Keep -ing...
繼續做～

Keep going.

繼續前進／繼續努力下去。

Keep talking.

繼續說。

Keep practicing your speech. *practice* 練習

繼續練習你的演講。

Keep walking.

繼續走。

Keep running.

繼續跑。

 寫寫看

Keep

Things
I need to do right now.

我現在需要做的事。

清空與填滿

請寫下你想改正的不良嗜好、壞習慣或傾向，
並下定決心從今天起一一拋棄。
也請寫下你想開始養成的好習慣。

● 想改掉的習慣 ●

一直摸頭髮
的習慣

● 想養成的習慣 ●

在工作或
學習時
做筆記的習慣

WEEK 4

需要安慰
的時候

沒有人是完美的

◆ ◆ ◆

Did I make a stupid mistake?
Did I say something dumb?
How come I keep asking myself
those questions to make sure
that I didn't mess up?
It's all right. Nothing went wrong.
I did what I was supposed to do.
I don't have to act too careful around people.
After all, no one's perfect.

•

我是不是犯了一個愚蠢的錯誤？
我是不是說了什麼傻話？
我怎麼會不斷地問自己這樣的問題，
只為確認自己沒有搞砸？
沒關係的。沒有任何事情出錯。
我只是做了自己該做的事。
沒必要處處看他人的眼色，過於小心翼翼。
畢竟沒有人是完美的。

🌸 手寫體書寫

It's all right. Nothing went wrong. After all,
no one's perfect.

dumb 愚蠢的　*make sure* 弄清楚　*mess up* 做錯、搞砸

How come...?

怎麼～？

How come you never called me?

你怎麼從不打電話給我？

How come you're so late?

你怎麼這麼晚才來？

How come I didn't know about this?

我怎麼完全不知道這件事？

How come you told him but not me?

為什麼你告訴他，卻沒告訴我？

How come John didn't take the advice?

約翰為何不接受這個提議？

 寫寫看

How come

80

No one's perfect.

沒有人是完美的。

DAY
17

需要安慰的那種日子

◆ ◆ ◆

So often I have to fight back tears
and try hard not to show any weakness.
Who would ever want to make themselves
look vulnerable?
It's just one of those days.
But tomorrow will be another day.
I did so well today,
and I will do well again tomorrow.
I'd like to give myself a pat on the back.
I deserve it.

◆

我經常努力忍住不哭。
並為了不暴露任何弱點而竭盡全力。
誰又會願意讓自己顯得脆弱不堪？
今天也只是諸事不順的日子之一。
但明天又會是嶄新的一天。
今天我做得很好，明天我也會做得很好。
我想輕拍自己的背以示表揚，因為那是我應得的。

_____

_____

_____

_____

_____

_____

_____

_____

_____

🌸 手寫體書寫

I'd like to give myself a pat on the back.

I deserve it.

_____

_____

weakness 弱點　*vulnerable* 容易受傷的、脆弱的　*pat* 輕拍

Who would ever want to...?

誰會想～？

Who would ever want to do that?

這世上誰會想那樣做？

Who would ever want to live here?

誰會想住在這裡？

Who would ever want to work here?

誰會想在這裡工作？

Who would ever want to be their friend?

誰會想當他們的朋友？

Who would ever want to talk with him?

誰會想跟他說話？

 寫寫看

Who would ever want to

It's just one of those days.

今天也只是
諸事不順的日子之一。

偶爾瘋狂一下也不錯

· · ·

Life is one damn thing after another.
**So it wouldn't hurt if we do something
crazy once in a while,**
like escaping from our boring routines.
You might find yourself going overboard.
But what the heck. It won't hurt you that much.
Knock, knock.
You're only trying to wake yourself up.

人生充滿著一連串令人厭煩的事情。
所以偶爾做些瘋狂的事也沒什麼不好。
例如像逃離枯燥乏味的日常工作。
也許你會覺得那樣太過分了。
但那又怎麼樣。又不是什麼大不了的事。
叩叩。
你只不過是想喚醒自己罷了。

🌸 手寫體書寫

It wouldn't hurt if we do something crazy once in a while, like escaping from our boring routines.

routine 日常例行公事　*go overboard* 過分、超過、做過頭
what the heck 那又怎麼樣、管它的

It wouldn't hurt if...
即使～也不會出什麼大事

It wouldn't hurt if you give it a try.

嘗試一下也不會出什麼大事。

It wouldn't hurt if we buy some more food.

就算我們買多一點食物也沒什麼不好。

It wouldn't hurt if we eat out a little more often.

我們更常出去用餐也沒什麼不好。

It wouldn't hurt if we try a little harder.

我們再努力一點也沒什麼不好。

It wouldn't hurt if you listen to the advice.

你聽聽別人的建議也沒什麼壞處。

 寫寫看

It wouldn't hurt if

It's okay to act
a little crazy once in a while.

偶爾表現瘋狂一點也沒關係。

寶貴的逆耳忠言

◆ ◆ ◆

Sometimes you need critical advice.

No one likes to hear advice.

**What you *want* to hear may not always
be the same as what you *need* to hear.**

You can get lost if you just keep following
those sweet words.

About those who'd bother you with bitter advice,
it would be better to keep them close to you.

In most cases, they're the ones
you need to grow up.

Take my word for it.

·

有時你需要嚴厲的忠告。

儘管沒有人喜歡聽忠告。

但你「想聽」的話與你「需要聽」的話並非總是相同。

如果只聽從那些甜言蜜語，你可能會迷失方向。

最好將那些以逆耳忠言惹惱你的人留在身邊。

這些人通常是你成長時所需要的。

我向你保證。

🌸 手寫體書寫

What you want to hear may not always be the same as what you need to hear.

critical 批判性的、嚴謹的、挑剔的　*bitter* 苦的、激烈的
take one's word for it 相信某人的話

It would be better to...
〜會更好。

It would be better to take the bus.

搭公車可能會更好。

It would be better to ask first.

最好先問一下。

It would be better to stay home.

待在家裡會更好。

It would be better to leave early.

提早離開會更好。

It would be better to cancel the event.

取消活動會更好。

 寫寫看

It would be better to

You can get lost if you just keep following those sweet words.

如果只聽從那些甜言蜜語，你可能會迷失方向。

與生活保持距離

◆ ◆ ◆

Things may look quite different from a distance.
What they truly are may not be the same
as what they look like.
**So when things look blurry,
why not try to keep a certain distance
from all those events in life?**
Then you will feel more relaxed and
be able to save your tears for later, much later,
when the rain begins to fall.

從遠處，一切看起來可能有所不同。
有些事情實際上可能與我們看到的不一樣。
因此當它們看起來模糊不清時，何不試著與生活中的一切保持距離呢？
那麼，你也會變得輕鬆許多。
而且你可以將眼淚保留到很久，很久以後，
當雨開始落下時。

🌸 手寫體書寫

When things look blurry, why not try to keep a certain distance from all those events in life?

blurry 模糊的、不清楚的   *distance* 距離

Things look...

情況看起來～

Things look pretty serious to me.

在我看來，情況相當嚴峻。

Things look pretty positive to me.

在我看來，情況非常樂觀。

Things look gloomy right now.

目前情況看起來十分悲觀。

Things look great!

看起來非常好！

Things look bleak.　*bleak* 慘淡的、絕望的

情況看起來很慘淡。

 寫寫看

Things look

Things may look quite different
from a distance.

從遠處，一切看起來可能有所不同。

How to De-stress Myself
我自己的舒壓方式

當你感到煩躁或壓力大時，你會如何舒解壓力？
請在空白處寫下「我自己的舒壓方式」。

吃辛辣的
食物以及甜點

用熱水泡腳
緩解疲勞

送自己
小禮物
（八百元以下）

WEEK 5

相信自己
的習慣

我的救贖者正是自己

Do you sometimes feel that you're in need of help?
You should know that
only you can save yourself. No one else.
And it takes lots of courage to do that.
Anyone can be that courageous.
For sure, you are brave enough to break the shell
and see the world out there.
You may not be a superhero sent to save the world.
But you are brave and strong enough to save
at least one person: yourself.

你是否有時覺得自己需要幫助呢？
要知道，沒有人可以拯救你，只有你才能拯救自己。
而這需要極大的勇氣。
每個人都可以變得那麼勇敢。
你必然也有足夠的勇氣，可以打破外殼並見識到外面的世界。
或許你不是被派來拯救世界的超級英雄。
但你至少足夠堅強勇敢去拯救一個人：你自己。

手寫體書寫

But you are brave and strong enough to save at least one person: yourself.

courageous 有勇氣的　*shell* 外殼、殼

It takes lots of... to...

想要～需要很多～

It takes lots of patience to succeed.

想成功需要很有耐心。

It takes lots of time to do that.

需要花很多時間才能做到。

It takes lots of courage to propose.

求婚需要很大的勇氣。

It takes lots of effort to improve your English.

想學好英語需要付出很多努力。

It takes lots of guts to tell the truth.

想說真話需要很大的膽量。

 寫寫看

It takes lots of   to

Anyone can be that courageous.

每個人都可以變得那麼勇敢。

為了自己的小習慣

◆ ◆ ◆

Start to take on one good habit a day.

Memorize one new English word.

Laugh out loud ten times a day.

Walk up at least one flight of stairs.

Write a three-liner journal. It doesn't have to be long.

And it's okay to give up in just three days.

You can start again the next day.

Happiness doesn't have to be found

only at the end of the rainbow.

It's something we can find along the way.

Those small things in life will add up.

試著每天開始養成一項好習慣。
每天記一個新的英文單字、
每天放聲大笑十次、至少爬一層樓梯。
寫三行日記，不需要很長。
即使三天就放棄也沒關係。
只要隔天再重新開始就行了。
幸福不一定只在彩虹盡頭才能發現。
在前往的沿路上，也能找到某種幸福。
而那些生活中的小確幸會逐漸累積起來。

🌸 手寫體書寫

Happiness doesn't have to be found only at the end of the rainbow.

flight 樓梯　*journal* 日記　*add up* 累積

It doesn't have to be...
不一定要～

It doesn't have to be too spacious.   *spacious*（房間等）寬敞的

空間不一定要很寬敞。

It doesn't have to be glamourous.

不需要太華麗。

It doesn't have to be pretty.

不一定要很漂亮。

It doesn't have to be too wide.

沒必要太寬。

It doesn't have to be expensive.

不一定要價值昂貴。

 寫寫看

It doesn't have to be

Happiness can be found anywhere, everywhere.

幸福隨處可尋。

期待下次機會

Those many opportunities
that I chose not to grab
could've turned into something awesome.
Still, I have no regrets,
for I always believe in my choices.
**But next time, I will give it a shot
and see how it goes.
I'll be ready when opportunity knocks.**

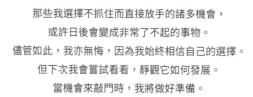

那些我選擇不抓住而直接放手的諸多機會，
或許日後會變成非常了不起的事物。
儘管如此，我亦無悔，因為我始終相信自己的選擇。
但下次我會嘗試看看，靜觀它如何發展。
當機會來敲門時，我將做好準備。

🌸 手寫體書寫

But next time, I will give it a shot and see how it goes. I'll be ready when opportunity knocks.

grab 抓住　*awesome* 了不起的、很好的　*give it a shot* 試一試

I chose not to...
我決定不～

I chose not to go there.

我決定不去那裡。

I chose not to go out today.

我決定今天不出門。

I chose not to take the offer.

我決定不接受那個提議。

I chose not to visit NASA this time.

我決定這次不造訪美國太空總署。

I chose not to see her tonight.

我決定今晚不與她見面。

 寫寫看

I chose not to

I'll be ready.

我將做好準備。

成功之日終將到來

♦ ♦ ♦

When will this darkness end?

Will this ever go away? I don't know.

But I know one thing for sure.

If I keep my chin up, things will pick up

sooner rather than later.

So I'll hang in there.

I'll never give up because I know I'll make it.

As a matter of fact, I AM pretty good at it.

這黑暗何時才會結束？

它會有消失的一天嗎？我不清楚。

但我確信一件事。

如果我繼續抬頭挺胸堅持下去，情況很會好轉。

所以我會堅持下去。

我絕不放棄，因為我知道我終將成功。

事實上，我還挺擅長堅持的。

🌸 手寫體書寫

If I keep my chin up, things will pick up sooner rather than later. So I'll hang in there.

pick up 好轉　　*make it* 做到、成功

... go away ...
消失／遠離／離開

This syrup will make the pain **go away**.

這個糖漿能消除疼痛。

Jane has **gone away** for a month.

距離珍離開已經過一個月了。

Please **go away** and leave me alone.

拜託你走開，讓我一個人靜一靜。

I might be **going away** this weekend.

我這個週末可能會出去一趟。

We're **going away** for vacation.

我們要去度假。

🌸 寫寫看

go away

That day will come.

那天遲早會到來。

目標從設定那一刻起開始實現

◆ ◆ ◆

Where do you see yourself in the future?
Try to answer these questions one by one.
What goals do you hope to achieve in your lifetime;
in the month, in five years, or in ten years?
How about… in an hour?
Those goals don't have to be grandiose.
**Every simple and small goal counts as long as
it drives you forward.**

未來的你會變得如何呢？
請試著一一回答這些問題。
你人生中想達成的目標是什麼？
你這個月的目標、五年後的目標、十年後的目標是什麼？
那一小時後的目標又是什麼？
那些目標不一定要非常宏偉。
所有簡單的小目標，只要能推動你前進，
便具有意義。

❀ 手寫體書寫

Every simple and small goal counts as long as it drives you forward.

achieve 成就　*grandiose* 宏偉的　*count* 重要、有意義

Every... counts.

所有～都很重要。

Every experience **counts.**

所有經驗都很重要。

Every vote **counts.**　　*vote* 選票

每一票都很重要。

Every opinion **counts.**

所有意見都一樣重要。

Every minute **counts.**

每一分鐘都很重要。

Everybody **counts.**

所有人都很重要。

 寫寫看

Every _____ counts.

Let's go up!

我們上去吧！

My Goals
我一定要實現的目標

請寫下你想於一年、三年、五年後達成的目標。
確認這些目標是否實現，將有助於你設定新目標。

• 一年後的目標 •

• 三年後的目標 •

• 五年後的目標 •

WEEK 6

再次，
去愛吧

我要投入名為你的冒險之中

◆ ◆ ◆

When I look around, I see you everywhere.
Whatever I lay my eyes on, **there's always you,**
cheering me up as my biggest fan.
Then I just whisper to myself,
"I will be your biggest cheerleader, too."
I'm not too sure if we're meant to be.
But for now, I know what I want,
and I'm willing to take the chance.

•

當我環顧四周，到處都能見到你。
我目光所及之處，總有你的身影，
作為最熱情的粉絲支持我。
於是，我亦在心中低語：
「我也會成為你最忠實的支持者。」
我無法完全確定，我們是否命中註定。
但我知道自己現在想要什麼，
而我願意放手一搏、冒險一次。

🌸 手寫體書寫

There's always you, cheering me up as my biggest fan. I will be your biggest cheerleader, too.

cheer ~ up 為～打氣　*whisper* 輕聲低語　*chance* 機會、可能性

I'm willing to...
我很樂意～

I'm willing to help you.

我很樂意幫助你。

I'm willing to follow your advice.

我願意聽從你的建議。

I'm willing to move to a different country.

我有意移居到其他國家。

I'm willing to take the job offer.

我有意接受工作邀約。

I'm willing to change seats with you.

我很樂意和你換位置。

 寫寫看

I'm willing to

I'm falling into you.

我愛上了你。

愛情很奇怪

♦ ♦ ♦

When in love, I get to lose myself.

All I think of is nothing but him/her.

Honestly, I'm not happy being like that.

Every time I fall in love, I become a fool,

but I can't seem to help it.

Maybe it's due to the incomparable and

irresistible excitement that love brings.

And I can't seem to get enough of it.

當我墜入愛河時，就會迷失自我。

滿腦子想的都是那個人。

老實說，我也不喜歡自己那種樣子。

每次墜入愛河時，我就會變成傻瓜，但我亦無能為力。

或許是因為愛情帶來了無與倫比、難以抗拒的快感。

而那種激情不會令人厭倦。

🌸 手寫體書寫

Every time I fall in love, I become a fool, but
I can't seem to help it.

---

can't help it 無能為力   *incomparable* 無與倫比的   *irresistible* 無法抗拒的

I'm not happy -ing...
我不喜歡～

I'm not happy working like this.

我不喜歡這樣工作。

I'm not happy staying home all day.

我不喜歡整天待在家。

I'm not happy feeling tired all the time.

我不喜歡總是感到疲倦。

I'm not happy being stuck here.

被困在這裡的感覺很糟。

I'm not happy talking about my problems.

我不喜歡談論我的問題。

 寫寫看

I'm not happy

Love is so strange.

愛情很奇怪。

有人為我付出

◆ ◆ ◆

I used to think that I had no real friends.
But I came to see that
there have always been some people
who have never given up on me.
Maybe I was looking in the wrong direction,
never listening to their whispers.
Today, I thank them
for being there for me all the time.

從前，我以為我沒有真正的朋友。
但後來發現了，有些人總在我身邊，
從來沒放棄過我。
或許是我一直看著錯誤的方向，
沒有傾聽他們的低語。
今天，我要感謝那些一直在我身邊，給予我力量的人。

🌸 手寫體書寫

But I came to see that there have always been some people who have never given up on me.

give up on 放棄對～的希望　　*be there for* 在～身邊給予力量

I used to...
我以前曾經～

I used to enjoy wine a lot.

我以前非常喜歡紅酒。

I used to think that Jane liked me.

我從前以為珍喜歡我。

I used to live in Jeju.

我以前住在濟州島。

I used to eat out a lot.

我以前經常出去吃飯。

I used to play baseball.

我曾經打過棒球。

 寫寫看

I used to

132

Hello, my friend.

嗨，我的朋友。

儘管悲傷，但到此為止吧

* * *

I did my best,

and I know you did your best

to make this work, too.

But there are things we cannot do anything about

no matter how hard we try.

I accept that we are not meant to be.

Though I'm sad to see our love fade away,

I wish you all the best.

為了我們的愛情，我已經盡力了，

而我知道你也盡力了。

然而，有些事無論我們如何努力也無可奈何。

我打算接受我們不是命中註定的事實。

儘管眼見我們的愛情逐漸凋零令人悲傷，

我仍願你一切安好。

手寫體書寫

I accept that we are not meant to be.

do one's best 竭盡全力　*fade away* 逐漸消失
all the best （問候語）祝好運、祝一切安好

We're meant to...
我們註定要～

We're meant to work together.

我們註定要一起工作。

We're meant to love each other.

我們註定要彼此相愛。

We're meant to be together.

我們註定要在一起。

We're meant to come here again.

我們註定要再次來到這裡。

We're meant to live together.

我們註定要一起生活。

 寫寫看

We're meant to

This must be it, but...

應該就此結束了，但是……

擁抱依然思念的心

◆ ◆ ◆

I miss you. No doubt.
I do nothing but miss you,
and that's how I spend my time.
After all this suffering,
I know a new phase will begin for me.
Losing you is heartbreaking,
but I will embrace it, too.

•

我想念你。這是毋庸置疑的。
我所有時間都只用來想你。
待這一切痛苦過去後，我知道我將開始一個新階段。
雖然失去你讓我心碎萬分，
但我將連那份苦楚一同擁抱。

❀ 手寫體書寫

After all this suffering, I know a new phase
will begin for me.

doubt 懷疑　*suffering* 痛苦　*embrace* 接受、擁抱

... nothing but...
除了～ 什麼也沒～

I did **nothing but** play games all day.

我整天都在玩遊戲。

We did **nothing but** cook meals.

我們除了煮飯沒做別的事。

I bought **nothing but** this hat.

我只買了這頂帽子。

We sang **nothing but** love songs.

我們只唱情歌。

She said **nothing but** a short *hello*.

她沒說別的，只說了一聲「你好」。

🌸 寫寫看

nothing but

new phase

新階段

我最愛的事物

你真心珍惜和喜愛的是什麼？
請寫下你喜愛的人、物品、地點和動物等，並一同寫下理由。

- 儘管有時讓人討厭，但總是為我加油的家人。

- 一看到我就會搖著尾巴跑過來的小狗。

- 我家附近玫瑰盛開的公園。

-

-

-

-

-

-

WEEK 7

渺小而偉大
的挑戰

DAY

31

現在馬上行動！

✦ ✦ ✦

Do you miss someone? Just call.

Do you have a question? Just ask.

Do you love someone? Just tell that person.

Do you want to meet up with someone?

Just invite that person.

If you'd like to receive a letter from someone,

write that person a letter first.

Just do it.

You've done enough thinking already.

Now get up and move!

你有想念的人嗎？那就打電話吧。

你有問題想問嗎？那就問吧。

你愛著某人嗎？那就告訴那個人吧。

你想和某人見面嗎？那就邀請那個人吧。

如果你想收到某人的來信，就先寫信給那個人。

去做就對了。

你已經思考夠多了。

現在就站起來行動吧！

讀、聆聽、書寫

手寫體書寫

Just do it. You've done enough thinking already. Now get up and move!

---

meet up with 和～見面　　*receive* 收到

You've done enough -ing...

你已經～夠多了

You've done enough talking.

你已經說夠多了。

You've done enough trying.

你已經嘗試夠多了。

You've done enough waiting.

你已經等夠久了。

You've done enough guessing.

你已經猜夠多了。

You've done enough doubting.

你已經懷疑夠多了。

 寫寫看

You've done enough

146

The light's on. It's time.

燈亮了。是時候了。

上天也會幫助我的

I believe that heaven helps those
who help themselves.
If I just wait around and do nothing,
there'll never be another chance for me.
So I will get up now and give it another try.
Then finally, heaven will notice
and start helping me.

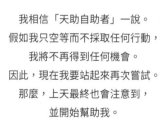

我相信「天助自助者」一說。
假如我只空等而不採取任何行動,
我將不再得到任何機會。
因此,現在我要站起來再次嘗試。
那麼,上天最終也會注意到,
並開始幫助我。

🌸 手寫體書寫

I will get up now and give it another try. Then finally, heaven will notice and start helping me.

wait around 空等著　*give it a try* 試一試

I believe...

我相信～

I believe we can get through this.   *get through* 渡過、熬過

我相信我們會渡過難關的。

I believe we should support one another.

我認為我們應互相扶持。

I believe they will like our idea.

相信他們一定會喜歡我們的點子。

I believe we can make a profit this month.

我相信我們這個月能夠獲利。

I believe I can get there in no time.

我想我很快就能抵達那裡了。

 寫寫看

I believe

150

Heaven helps me.

上天助我。

起霧的日子，
一步一步向前

I wish rain would come and wash away the dirt.
This blurry sight often frustrates me.
It's hard to look further ahead.
Nothing much is in sight.
So I decide to focus on
what's right in front of me for now
and take one step at a time.
Slowly and carefully.

真希望下場雨將泥土灰塵全部沖走。
模糊的視野經常讓我感到沮喪，
因為難以向前展望，幾乎什麼也看不見。
所以我決定現在要專注於眼前的事物，
接著一次邁出一步，
慢慢地，慎重地。

🌸 手寫體書寫

So I decide to focus on what's right in front of me for now and take one step at a time.

sight 視野、視線　*frustrate* 使氣餒、沮喪　*further* 更遠地

It's hard to...
難以～

It's hard to understand him.

難以理解他。

It's hard to tell how old she is.　*tell* 判斷

難以判斷她的年齡。

It's hard to believe that story.

那個故事令人難以致信。

It's hard to find time to see my friends.

難以抽出時間與我的朋友相見。

It's hard to keep calm all the time.

始終保持冷靜非常困難。

 寫寫看

It's hard to

One step at a time.

一次邁出一步。

承擔風險的覺悟

It takes a lot to stand up for myself
because I would have to take all the risks.
My reputation may be damaged.
I may lose some people.
**But those risks are worth taking
if I could speak up and stand up for myself.**
So never back down.

堅持自己立場是件相當困難的事，
因為一切風險都要自行承擔。
我的名譽可能會受損，甚至可能失去某些人。
但只要能挺身而出為自己發聲，
承擔那些風險便是值得的。
所以，絕對不要退縮。

🌸 手寫體書寫

But those risks are worth taking if I could
speak up and stand up for myself.

stand up for oneself 為自己發聲、勇敢抵抗
speak up for 為～辯護、講話　*back down* 退縮

be worth -ing...

值得～

The food there **was worth waiting** for.

那裡的食物值得一等。

The museum **is worth visiting**.

那間博物館值得一遊。

The house **was** not **worth buying**.

那棟房子不值得買。

There**'s** not much **worth reading**.

那沒什麼值得閱讀的。

It**'s worth checking** the details before you sign the contract.

在簽約前，先確認合約細節是值得的。

🌸 寫寫看

worth

Never back down.

永不退縮。

今天是「傾聽日」

‧‧‧

People can't wait to tell their own stories.
And they're not good at listening.
But what if, even for just one day,
we keep our mouths shut,
just listen to what others have to say
and keep our minds open, not just our ears.
I mean, wouldn't it be nice
if you had someone to talk to?
Tonight, we can all be that someone for others.

每個人都想訴說自己的故事，
且不擅長傾聽。
然而，哪怕只有一天，
若我們可以閉上嘴巴，傾聽別人的故事，
不只是打開耳朵，還要敞開心扉。
我的意思是，有個可以暢所欲言的人不是很好嗎？
今夜我們都可以成為，他人可以訴說真心話的那個人。

🌸 手寫體書寫

Just listen to what others have to say, and keep our minds open, not just our ears.

can't wait 迫不及待　*others* 其他人／東西

... can't wait to...

迫不及待想～

I **can't wait to** meet her.

我迫不及待想見她。

He **can't wait to** work with you soon.

他很期待與你合作。

I **can't wait to** visit the Eiffel Tower.

我很期待造訪艾菲爾鐵塔。

I **can't wait to** taste the pie!

我想快點嚐嚐那個派！

She **can't wait to** see the movie.

她迫不及待想看那部電影。

 寫寫看

can't wait to

Just listen for a day.

今天是傾聽日。

>>> *Bring It On!* <<<
放馬過來吧！

請每天從下面的清單中，選擇一項進行挑戰。
若挑戰成功，請在前面方格中打勾。

☐ 三十分鐘內不看手機

☐ 聽著冥想音樂為一天做總結

☐ 起床後喝一杯溫水

☐ 寫下一整首英語流行歌的歌詞

☐ 每兩小時做一次簡單的伸展運動

☐ 閱讀一篇英語童話故事

☐ 用英語寫三行日記

☐ 今天是徒步日！不要搭電梯

☐ 走五千步以上

WEEK 8

人生依然
如此美麗

專注於「此時此刻」

◆ ◆ ◆

Let's say there's a cup with a little water in it.
If you see the cup is still half full,
your mind is set in the future.
If you see the cup is already half empty,
your mind is set in the past.
**Why not just lift the cup
and drink the water right away?
Then your mind will be fully set
in the present.**

◆

假設有一個裝了少量水的杯子。
如果你認為杯子還是半滿的，
代表你把心思放在未來。
如果你認為杯子已經半空了，
代表你讓心思停留在過去。
何不直接拿起杯子喝掉那些水呢？
如此一來，你的心思便能完全專注在當下。

🌸 手寫體書寫

Why not just lift the cup and drink the water right away? Then your mind will be fully set in the present.

set 放置、使處於　*empty* 空的

Let's say...
假設～

Let's say it's winter right now.

假設現在是冬天。

Let's say we're a married couple.

假設我們是夫妻。

Let's say you want to quit your job.

假設你想辭職。

Let's say a movie has just started.

假設電影現在剛開始。

Let's say I'm your friend.

假設我是你的朋友。

 寫寫看

Let's say

here and now

此時此刻

各自不同的幸福樣貌

◆ ◆ ◆

To some people, big money can mean happiness.
To others, it's love that brings them happiness.
**Happiness comes in all different shapes
and sizes.** And it's up to you
to decide which one to choose.
Isn't that a good enough reason for us to stop
comparing ourselves to others?
Trying to keep up with the Joneses
will never get you anywhere.
Find your own happiness.

對某些人來說，財富意味著幸福。
對另一些人來說，是愛為他們帶來幸福。
幸福以各種不同樣貌出現。
要選擇其中哪一種，取決於你。
這不正是讓我們停止與他人比較的一個好理由嗎？
一味追逐他人背影是毫無意義的。
去尋找屬於自己的幸福吧。

手寫體書寫

Happiness comes in all different shapes and sizes. Find your own happiness.

be up to 取決於～
keep up with the Joneses （在物質生活方面）與朋友或鄰居比較

... come in all different shapes and sizes.
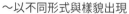
～以不同形式與樣貌出現

These pants **come in all different shapes and sizes.**

這些褲子都有不同的款式和尺寸。

This blouse **comes in all different shapes and sizes.**

這件襯衫有不同的款式和尺寸。

Houses here **come in all different shapes and sizes.**

這裡的房子格局和大小都不一樣。

Family **comes in all different shapes and sizes.**

家庭的形態和規模各不相同。

Colleges **come in all different shapes and sizes.**

大學有不同的形式和規模。

 寫寫看

come in all different shapes and sizes.

Happiness
comes in all different shapes and sizes.

幸福以各種不同樣貌出現。

我是書寫自己人生的作家

Imagine yourself writing your own biography
someday way into the future,
looking at yourself as a teenager
and then in your 20s, 30s, and 40s…
How would you like to be described at those times?
In a glamorous way like the vivid colors
of the rainbow or in a rather soft yet
subtle way like hazy water in a lake?
**Today will be the first chapter
and tomorrow the second.**
So let's try to make the best out of our times!

想像一下，在遙遠未來的某一天正在書寫自傳的你。
看著20幾歲、30幾歲和40幾歲的自己……
你希望那時候的自己被如何描述？
是如同鮮豔彩虹般絢麗多彩？
亦或像霧濛濛的湖水一樣柔和而細緻？
今天將成為第一章，明天則是第二章。
因此，讓我們努力打造最美好的時光吧！

手寫體書寫

Today will be the first chapter and tomorrow the second.

biography 生平傳記　glamorous 華麗的　vivid 鮮明的　hazy 霧濛濛的

Imagine yourself -ing...
想像一下在～的你

Imagine yourself working here.

想像一下在這裡工作的你。

Imagine yourself enjoying a vacation on the beach.

想像一下在海邊度假的你。

Imagine yourself living in this house.

想像一下住在這棟房子的你。

Imagine yourself speaking on this stage.

想像一下在這個舞臺上發言的你。

Imagine yourself helping others.

想像一下幫助他人的你。

 寫寫看

Imagine yourself

Life is what you make of it.

人生是由自己創造的。

所謂的瀟灑生活

◆ ◆ ◆

Do you need to be "cool" all the time?

I'd rather face my true feelings and

take them as they are than be pretentious.

If you keep trying to put on the "cool look,"

it'll only eat you up from the inside.

So why not just admit your anger and

embarrassment and move on from there?

We do not need fake coolness to live a good life.

That's the real truth about being cool.

你一定要隨時都保持很「酷」嗎？

與其裝模作樣，我寧願正視自己的真實感受，

並接受它們原本的模樣。

如果你一直努力「故作瀟灑」，

只會讓內在逐漸被侵蝕。

所以何不乾脆大方承認自己的憤怒與窘迫，

然後重新開始呢？

我們不需要為了過得好而「裝酷」。

這才是「酷」的真正本質。

🌸 手寫體書寫

So why not just admit your anger and

embarrassment and move on from there?

---

pretentious 裝模作樣的　　*admit* 承認　　*embarrassment* 尷尬、困窘

I'd rather...

我寧願～

I'd rather take the bus.

我寧願搭公車。

I'd rather stay home.

我寧願待在家。

I'd rather have some tea.　　*have* 吃、喝

我寧願喝茶。

I'd rather not eat at all.

我寧願什麼都不吃。

I'd rather not try it.

我寧願不去嘗試。

 寫寫看

I'd rather

You know what?
I'm NOT cool.

你知道嗎？
我並「不」酷。

比今天更好的我

♦ ♦ ♦

Who do I compete against?
Do I have a rival to fight against?
Do I have anyone that I want to beat?
Is there any point in a rivalry?
Not really.
I only have myself of yesterday to compare with.
**If I got better in any sense today,
that makes me a true winner.**

我在跟誰競爭？
我有需要對抗的對手嗎？
我有想要打敗的對象嗎？
相互較勁有什麼意義呢？
事實上，並沒有。
因為我唯一需要比較的，只有昨日的自己。
無論從任何層面，只要今天的我有所進步，
那便會使我成為真正的贏家。

🌸 讀、聆聽、書寫

_____

_____

_____

_____

_____

_____

_____

_____

_____

🌸 手寫體書寫

If I got better in any sense today, that makes me a true winner.

_____

_____

compete 競爭 *beat* 打敗 *sense* 意義

Is there any point in…?
～有什麼用？

Is there any point in doing the survey?

做問卷調查有用嗎？

Is there any point in learning this language?

學習這門語言有用嗎？

Is there any point in getting a driver's license?

取得駕照有什麼意義嗎？

Is there any point in buying stocks now?

現在買股票有什麼意義嗎？

Is there any point in cleaning this place?

打掃此地有什麼意義嗎？

🌸 寫寫看

Is there any point in

Nice to meet a better me.

很高興見到你，更好的我。

我的願望清單

「bucket list」指的是記錄一個人想做或必須完成事項的清單。
請寫下你想要實現的願望清單。

- 在埃及金字塔前拍照

- 玩高空彈跳

- 學鋼琴

- 和父母去海外旅行

-

-

-

-

-

Famous Quotes

想抄錄的
十二則英語名言

—• 01 •—

Paradise is where I am.

我所在的地方即為天堂。

by Voltaire

—• 02 •—

It is impossible to live without failing at something unless you live so cautiously that you might as well not have lived at all–in which case, you fail by default.

生活不可能不經歷失敗，除非你謹慎得想避開失敗。
但這麼小心翼翼的人生，即便沒失敗過，
其實本質上也是一種失敗。

by J.K. Rowling

—• 03 •—

You only live once,
but if you do it right, once is enough.

人生只有一次，
但若活得精彩，一次也足夠了。

by Mae West

I've learned that people will forget what you said,
people will forget what you did, but people will never
forget how you made them feel.

我發現人們會忘記你說過的話和做過的事。
但人們永遠不會忘記你帶給他們的感受。

by Maya Angelou

—— · *05* · ——

Don't walk in front of me. I may not follow.
Don't walk behind me. I may not lead.
Walk beside me… Just be my friend.

別走在我前面。我可能會跟不上。
別走在我後面。我可能不會帶路。
請走在我身邊，當我的朋友就好。

by Albert Camus

—— · *06* · ——

Darkness cannot drive out darkness;
only light can do that. Hate cannot drive out hate;
only love can do that.

黑暗無法驅逐黑暗；唯有光明可以。
仇恨無法泯滅仇恨；唯有愛才可以。

by Martin Luther King Jr.

It is better to be hated for what you are
than to be loved for what you are not.

因你的真實而被討厭，
好過因你的虛偽而被愛。

by Andre Gide

You know you're in love
when you can't fall asleep
because reality is finally better than your dreams.

當你無法入睡時，你就知道你戀愛了。
因為現實終於比夢境更美好。

by Dr. Seuss

Imperfection is beauty, madness is genius
and it's better to be absolutely ridiculous
than absolutely boring.

不完美是一種美，瘋狂是一種天賦。
荒唐無稽總好過無聊至極。

by Marilyn Monroe

There are only two ways to live your life.
One is as though nothing is a miracle.
The other is as though everything is a miracle.

有兩種生活方式。
一種是相信凡事沒有奇蹟。
另一種是將凡事都當成奇蹟。

by Albert Einstein

Be yourself; everyone else is already taken.

做你自己吧；其他角色都已經有人扮演了。

by Oscar Wilde

It is what you read when you don't have to that
determines what you will be when you can't help it.

你在非必要時所閱讀的內容，
將決定你在別無選擇的情況下會成為什麼樣的人。

by Oscar Wilde

EZ TALK

英語療癒筆記：每天手寫10分鐘的幸福時光

作　　者：李寶寧
譯　　者：韓蔚笙
主　　編：潘亭軒
責任編輯：鄭雅方
封面插畫：楊亦玄
封面設計：蕭旭芳
內頁排版：簡單瑛設
行銷企劃：張爾芸

發 行 人：洪祺祥
副總經理：洪偉傑
副總編輯：曹仲堯
法律顧問：建大法律事務所
財務顧問：高威會計師事務所

出　　版：日月文化出版股份有限公司
製　　作：EZ叢書館
地　　址：臺北市信義路三段151號8樓
電　　話：(02)2708-5509
傳　　真：(02)2708-6157
客服信箱：service@heliopolis.com.tw
網　　址：www.heliopolis.com.tw
郵撥帳號：19716071日月文化出版股份有限公司

總 經 銷：聯合發行股份有限公司
電　　話：(02)2917-8022
傳　　真：(02)2915-7212
印　　刷：中原造像股份有限公司
初　　版：2024年8月
定　　價：380元
I S B N：978-626-7405-94-9

英語療癒筆記：每天手寫10分鐘的幸福時光 / 李寶寧
著；韓蔚笙譯. – 初版. – 臺北市：日月文化出版股份
有限公司, 2024.08
192面；14.7 x 21公分
ISBN 978-626-7405-94-9（平裝）
1.CST: 自我實現　2.CST: 生活指導　3.CST: 英語
177.2　　　　　　　　　　　　　　113007847